The Incredible Mason Bee book

Written by
Steven and Catherine Scanlan

Edition 1

i

The Incredible Mason Bee book

First Published in Duncan, Vancouver Island, 2021

ISBN: 978-1-989681-09-1

Text and Graphics, Copyright of Steven Scanlan, 2021

A Catalogue entry for the title and name of this book reside with the Canadian Registry of ISBN

All rights reserved. No part of this publication may be reproduced, stored in a retrieval system, or transmitted in any form or by any means, electronic, mechanical, photocopying, recording or otherwise, without the prior written agreement of Steven Scanlan.

ISLAND BOOKS

We dedicate this book to the memory of

Eugene Fleck

Gentleman, friend, scholar, and mason bee master.

v

Table of Contents

Preface .... *viii*
Our Story .... *xi*
Introduction 1
What is Pollination? 4
The Mason Bee 6
The Mason Bee Life Cycle 9
    Spring 9
    Summer 10
    Fall 11
    Winter 12
Types of Mason Bee Housing 13
    Reed Houses 14
        Advantages of Reed Houses 15
        Concerns with Reed Houses 15
    Paper Straw Houses 15
        Advantages of Paper Straw Houses 16
        Concerns with Paper Straw Houses 17
    Drilled Hole Houses 17
        Concerns with Drilled Hole Houses 18
    Separable Tray Houses 19
        Advantages of Separable Tray Houses 19
        Concerns with Separable Tray Houses 19
Make Your Own Mason Bee House 21
    How to Make a Reed House 23
    How to Make a Paper Straw House 24

How to make a Drilled Hole House 27

The Beekeeper Calendar 35

  Spring 35
    Activity: Siting Your Mason Bee House (March-April) 35
    Activity: Introducing the cocoons to the housing 36

  Summer 39
    Activity: Taking Down Your Mason Bee House (August) 40

  Fall 41
    Activity: Cleaning and Harvesting the Cocoons (October) 41

  Winter 53

Chapter 7 54

Cleaning a Paper Straw House 54

Pests and Diseases 56

  General Garden Pests 57

  Pests from Spring to Fall 58

  Pests During the Fall 60

Bee-Attracting Plants 63

  Suggested Plantings 64
    Plants and Flowers 64
    Trees 65

Conclusion 66

References I
    Spring Calendar II
    Summer Calendar III
    Fall Calendar IV

Figures and Pictures V

Preface

Think back to when you were younger. If you can remember the 1980s through to 2000, you may recall driving along the road for long distances and pulling over to get gas. Before you filled the gas tank, you may have grabbed a squeegee and sponged the windscreen to clear off the bugs, flies, bees, and other odd insects that accumulated there over the course of the journey. Amongst these splatters on the windscreen were some of the pollinators who worked at spreading pollen across trees and plants, and supported our gardens and farms with producing flowers, trees, fruits, and vegetables (*Figure 1*).

Figure 1: A bumblebee pollinating a flower.

Now consider the last time you cleaned your windscreen. Can you remember? If you can, it was probably a special occasion and not the daily event it used to be.

During recent years, changes in farming practice and home garden maintenance has accelerated the destruction of pollinator populations. "The main threats facing pollinators are habitat loss, degradation and fragmentation of safe areas to lay their eggs. As native vegetation is replaced by roadways, manicured lawns, crops and non-native gardens, pollinators lose the food and nesting sites that are necessary for their survival." [i]

Over recent years the world has introduced pesticides to kill destructive insects and protect our plants and crops. The consequence of these actions is we have accidentally damaged or killed important pollinators in the process of deployment. Farms utilize pesticides on a much larger scale than the average person—they spray enormous amounts across their land to increase yield, but inadvertently destroy the very insects they wish to encourage.

Plant choice can also have a role in pollinator populations. Large swaths of plants that produce minimal pollen, such as grasses and some genetically modified flowers, force pollinators away from the garden. Changes in the development of modern farming techniques has reduced the frequency and complexity of hedgerows, such as the great plains of Manitoba and Saskatchewan, which have vast fields of grain-bearing plants covering the land with no boundaries or hedgerows between them.

The destruction of hedgerow borders to the very edge of the field further reduce the number of free flowers, wildflowers, and other plants that pollinators depend upon, as well as insects crucial to sustaining the ecosystem.

Pollinators are an important part of our garden and our lives; it is estimated that over 30% of all the food we eat are pollinated by these insects[ii]. If pollinators disappear, vegetation health drastically suffers; we would lose access to our favourite flowers, fruits, nuts, and vegetables. Plant-based items would also become less abundant. There would be a dramatic change in how we farm, what we eat and how we fare.

The extent of the damage to pollinator populations is yet to be fully realized, but evidence [iii] shows there will be a severe change in the way we address pollination. Some parts of Asia have become so polluted with pesticides that now use people, full time, to pollinate trees and flowers by hand [iii].

In Saskatchewan and Manitoba, farmers commonly bring hives containing millions of honeybees across the country, or even internationally, to pollinate their fields [iv]. What has happened to the local pollinators in these places to require such extreme measures? This question will become the norm unless we work as a community to amend the way we manage our gardens and our farming practices.

Across the world, with the growing realization of the importance of bees, wasps, butterflies and birds in the pollination process, more people are working to take better care of their gardens.

In some countries the use of the more destructive pesticides is being banned to enable pollinators to flourish once more and hopefully redress the balance before it is too late [iii].

Our Story

Our interest in the mason bee began when we attended a lecture at our local college. Eugene Fleck, a local beekeeper, presented the story of the mason bee and its immediate impact on gardens and outlined the part the bee played in the greater food production. We were engrossed, and after a year of working with these fascinating and important bees we decided to commit to changing how we manage our own garden and informing the wider community as to the benefits and advantages of keeping mason bees.

As a result of meeting Eugene, we decided that we could make a difference with mason bees in our own neighbourhood and started Long Live Bees (LLB). As a result of this venture, we have successfully introduced hundreds of people and farms to keeping their own mason bees and now advise on how to improve mason bee population in their own neighbourhoods. Long Live bees has subsequently expanded to include other gifts, books, services, and training with a percentage of the earnings going to benefit Canadian bee research funds.

This book explains how to keep and enjoy mason bees, based on the lessons that Eugene originally shared in his lectures. We have added some additional content to explain why we consider mason bees survival essential to all our futures and information on current pressures in gardens, crops, farms, and produce.

This book is partly informative, and partly a record of your year with the mason bee. It is an opportunity to maintain a calendar of successes and any challenges you have faced to allow you to be more successful in subsequent years. Add photos, thoughts, ideas, observations, and issues to make the most of your mason bee keeping experience.

Introduction

The mason bee is a solitary bee which dedicating it's life to laying eggs and ensuring that there is enough pollen for their larva to feed on, thus, increasing the chances of the successful growth of the larvae through to pupal stage and eventual hatching as an adult bee in the spring.

Unlike honeybees, who nest in hives with a queen, mason bees nest in individual holes and their only interaction with other mason bees is to mate. They work alone, but do not mind living and working in close proximity to other bees and insects. Their nest is solely their own environment, and as they do not cooperate with other bees concerning the nest's construction or the rearing of the brood, they are almost never aggressive.

Female mason bees have stingers, but they will only sting if they are trapped or squeezed; even so, their sting is nothing to fear, since the sting is more akin to a mosquito bite than the typical bee sting. Combined with the male's lack of stinger, mason bees are the ideal pollinator to introduce to your garden. It is still strongly advised that you do not keep mason bees if you suffer from anaphylaxis or any other type of allergy to bees.

The mason bee does not make honey in any form, but what it contributes to the pollination of fruit, vegetable and flower production far outweighs that of the honeybee in terms of productivity.

Mason bees occur in almost all regions of the northern hemisphere. More than 340 species of mason bee exist across the world, with approximately 140 species residing in North

America alone. Taxonomists place all North American mason bees in the genus Osmia, which is further subdivided into nine subgenera. The mason bee genus—together with the genus Megachile (leafcutter and resin bees) and a few other genera make up the family Megachilidae, the second largest family of bees in the world.[vi] The family is united by a unique abdominal structure called a scopa which is used to carry pollen. Most other bees that gather pollen, including the familiar honeybee, carry pollen in sacks, on their legs.

Mason bees earn their name from the way the female protects her eggs. The female will form a mud wall at the back of the chosen hole. The wall is formed from mud and water collected from the ground. On completion of the wall, she will visit hundreds of flowers for their pollen and then lay her egg on top. After collecting enough pollen load the mason bee will build another wall, again using mud to block off and protect the egg cell.

Osmia lignaria (also known as the orchard mason bee or blue orchard bee) is the most common species of native mason bees found in the Pacific Northwest. Orchard mason bees look very similar to common house flies, with large black bodies and a dark blue iridescent sheen, (*Figure 2*). however, they bear an additional set of wings.

The orchard mason bee is from a family of solitary bees that do not maintain a hive or live in a commune. The mason bee's desire to live a solitary life means she does not have to help, support, or defend a large hive of tens of thousands of bees; neither does she need to work hard for other bees or find food for the queen. However, a solitary bee is unprotected by other bees and needs to collect her own pollen, protect her own young and nest, and locate a suitable home for her eggs on her own.

This native species is important in pollinating spring-blooming crops, and they are often placed in orchards ready to emerge in spring for pollination. The mason bee is an excellent pollinator, preferring fruit and nut trees but equally at home with other flower and pollen-bearing plants.

Figure 2: Mason bee entering a Reed House

Due to widespread declines of honeybees and native pollinators, mason bees can help diversify the range of pollinators in agricultural systems, bolstering the pollination rates and in some instances being the main pollinator for the spring/early summer seasons [vii].

Over recent years, farmers and commercial growers have introduced mason bees for pollination of large-scale commercial produce. Interest in the mason bee has steadily increased in recent years due to the economic importance of their super-pollination efforts, and their ease of care.

Taking care of native, non-stinging mason bees can be undertaken in almost all locations, even in cities and urban spaces. Keeping mason bees is an excellent way to help the local environment, and it's also an amazing, inexpensive, and educational project for young adults and children.

Chapter 1

What is Pollination?

To understand why Long Live Bees are so fascinated by the mason bee, we need to understand their function in our gardens. Many species of pollinators work in our gardens, collecting nectar and pollinating our flowers and trees. But what do we mean by pollination?

Pollination is the method by which a plant transports pollen from the male part of the flower to the female part of another similar plant. Pollination means the plant will be able to produce seeds in the new season. These seeds will also contain the genetic information necessary to reproduce.

Pollinators move pollen between an incredible number of plants. Pollinators are not limited to insects, but also can include wind and rain, birds, insects, bees, bats, butterflies, moths, and other small animals which visit flowers. Pollinators are attracted to plants by the scent or colour of the flower. Pollen can be very pungent, thus attracting the pollinator from wide distances. The plant can only produce when the pollen is transferred between flowers of the same type or species.

Pollination is a by-product of the pollinators primary focus, gathering pollen for food or shelter. When an insect pollinates, it is working hard to collect pollen for its eggs or young or feeding itself by sipping nectar from the flower. As a result, the pollen attaches to the insect body. When the mason bee visits another flower, pollen falls onto the flower's stigma (female part). This action results in the successful reproduction of a subsequent flower the following season.

Not all plants require a pollinator to produce their seeds. Some plants are self-pollinating. This means that the plant will fertilize itself without the aid of another plant or flower. It important to note that most plants are cross-pollinated and need another pollinator—obtaining the pollen from another plant.

Pollinators have a vital role in the productivity of plants. Without the pollinator, including mason bees, cross-pollinating plants struggle to reproduce (*Figure 3*).

Figure 3: Mason Bee collecting Pollen

As the incidence of pollination reduces due to loss of pollinators, it becomes likely that a plant will fail to reproduce. Failure in a plant's reproduction and pollination means the plant will not produce seed and fruit. This affects the flowers in our gardens, the fruit we eat, the ecosystem and much of our food supply.

Chapter 2

The Mason Bee

The mason bee belongs to the Osmia species of solitary bee. They live for a short period of time, usually just 6 weeks in early spring. The males exist solely to reproduce, the females are dedicated to the laying of eggs and have the responsibility of ensuring the successful next generation of mason bees, which she will not live to see hatch.

Unlike the more familiar honeybee which can live for 122 – 150 days, the mason bee has an extremely short lifespan of approximately 42 – 50 days. This makes for a particularly frenetic life, as it must complete its life work during that limited time. The bee's solitary nature means that it does not have to help, support, or defend a large hive of tens of thousands of bees. Neither does it need to work hard for other bees or find food for the queen. The disadvantage of being a solitary bee is that it is not protected by other bees; she will need to find and collect her own pollen, protect her own young and locate a suitable source of food and other elements to protect her eggs. She must also find a suitable clay mud source to build the walls, water to drink and not least find a suitable place to live.

The lifespan of the mason bee is very short. The male will live long enough to complete the mating with females, up to 2 weeks. The female will live a little longer, up to 6 weeks. We therefore see the females commencing their role of laying eggs and collecting pollen and nectar from the point they have completed their mating.

During the spring season the mason bee will seek flowers and pollen of various types. They have little preference over which flowers to choose, but will seek fruit trees first, and move to spring flowering plants and vegetables as they become available. The sole mission a female mason bee is to lay eggs. She needs pollen and nectar to begin this process. If everything she needs is close by her chosen nesting place then she will lay between 30-35 eggs in her 4–6-week life.

During her lifetime she will visit up to 75 flowers to gather one full batch of pollen for each of her eggs. She will need approximately 25 batches of pollen (1875 flowers) for one pollen load. Each egg will need one pollen load and will eventually be used by the larvae that emerges. The mason bee will lay 2-4 eggs each day and therefore visit 3750-7500 flowers each day, a mammoth task (*Figure 4*).

In her work to deliver pollen to her eggs she completes a significant role in the pollination of the garden. With her visits to 75 flowers on each trip, she is a tremendous pollinator. She is far superior to other pollinators due to the way she collects the pollen, and the urgency with which she performs.

Figure 4: Mason Bee carrying pollen to the nest

The honeybee will be very clean when collecting the pollen, it will carefully collect the pollen and place it into sacs situated on its legs. The mason bee, by contrast, will bellyflop into the flower and roll around in the pollen covering her body. She will then move on to the next flower and repeat the action, depositing some pollen from the previous flowers.

Chapter 3

The Mason Bee Life Cycle

The mason bee life cycle follows alongside the yearly changing of the seasons. Each season, the mason bee enters a new stage of life and undertakes a series of new tasks.

The lifecycle starts with the egg laid in the spring, followed by the subsequent larva and growth period, pupation in the summer, transformation in the fall and dormancy over the winter and then finally hatching as an adult the following spring, starting the cycle once more.

Spring

At the commencement of the spring season, wild mason bee nests (which they make in open topped reeds, stalks, trees, or wooden house sidings) contain cocoons laid the previous spring, tightly packed behind individual mud walls. The cocoons have successfully survived hibernation through the winter snows and storms to awake in the spring. The season starts in the west of Canada and the United States during the month of March or April, dependant on the temperature of the world outside the safety of the nest. When the outside temperature reaches a comfortable 15 degrees, the males (the outside eggs of which were laid towards the front of the hole) will chew through their cocoons and exit their holes first. They will then wait around the nesting site for the females to emerge.

Females exit two days later, though they can take a little longer, depending upon the outside temperature. The bees require a temperature of at least 15deg C (60 deg F) for at least three consecutive days before the males will exit and two or more days after for the females to exit, providing the temperature remains above 15deg C. On exit from the hole the females will be immediately met by the males, and they will mate. The female then flies away from her hatching site for 24-48 hours to allow for fertilisation. The male's role is complete; and they die. Some will wait around the hole for a few more days in the hope more females will emerge.

Following the mating the females will search for a suitable site to lay their eggs, either in cracks in wooden siding, in hollow tubes, reeds or in purpose-built mason bee housing, usually returning to the site of their emergence. The hole she needs is 12-16cm (4.5 - 6 inch) long and an exact diameter of 8mm (5/16th inch).

Mason bees can choose the sex of the eggs they lay, and they do so the same way every time. She will lay the female eggs at the back of the hole, and the male eggs towards the front. The male eggs are laid at the front for two reasons:

1. The males exit first and need a clear way to leave. The males are more dispensable as not all of them are required to mate. Pests attacking the nest will eat the males at the front first, and not affect the more useful females in the back.

2. The mason bee lays more males than females to ensure that the females have a partner when they exit the nest the following spring.

Summer

Summer is a quiet time for both mason bee and beekeeper. The females will have completed their egg laying and will die. They will have laid between 2 or 3 eggs each day and a total of approximately 15-30 eggs through her lifespan of 5-7 weeks. In this short lifespan she will have rushed from flower to flower to collect enough pollen for her eggs and collect enough mud to build walls between each egg.

The egg will hatch and mature into a larva and will begin eating the pollen, they will fatten up over the course of the summer and settle into their hole and start to form the cocoon that will protect them through the winter months.

Do not look for mason bee activity around your nest at this time of year. Rather, around the beginning of May watch for the tubes' entrance as they are being capped with mud and the mason bee will search for another hole to lay her eggs. This is the sign that you have a successful nesting site. In July or August, the housing will need to be taken down and stored in a net bag in an unheated garage or shed. This will be covered in greater detail later.

Fall

During the fall, the bee larvae mature into adult bees surrounded by a tough cocoon. This takes several weeks to complete. They then enter a period of dormancy and continue to mature until it is time to wake the following spring.

There is minimal work for the mason beekeeper at this time of year but there is one important task that needs to be completed.

The housing will need to be cleaned (if you have housing which can be taken apart) and the cocoons harvested and stored throughout the winter. This ensures optimum survival rates for your bees. More on this in Chapter 6.

Winter

Through the winter the bee will lay dormant in hibernation within its cocoon and prepare for the spring when the whole cycle starts once more. There is no intervention necessary by the beekeeper.

Chapter 4

Types of Mason Bee Housing

Mason bees, in the wild, will lay their broods in small holes in the ground, trees, and other sheltered places. The bee is very particular about its nesting location and seeks a hole that is exactly 8 mm (5/16th inch) in diameter and 10–15 cm (4-6 inch) deep, with one end fully sealed. These dimensions are precise, and the bee will search a wider area for these exact measurements to lay it's eggs.

You can encourage mason bees to occupy your property by providing them with places to nest known as mason bee houses or mason bee condominiums. If the bees have many holes of the correct length and diameter available when they emerge from hibernation, they will be happy to move in and pollinate the surrounding plants for years to come.

Long Live Bees recommends helping mason bees in your garden by providing them with easily identifiable nests where they can quickly commence their egg laying. The advantage of providing a mason bee house is:

- Provides exactly the right accommodation quickly available to the emerging bees.
- Allows the mason beekeeper to protect the bee house through the most challenging period for the bees.
- Maximises the survival prospects of the bees by the intervention of the keeper's correct management.

- Protects the cocoon from the harsh winter weather.
- Reduces the risk of predators attacking the bees.

Four main styles of mason bee houses are available: a. reeds, b. paper straws, c. drilled holes, and d. separable trays. Each style has benefits that enable the mason bee to lay their eggs and produce several larvae, however some designs have more issues in management than others.

Reed Houses

Reed houses are available online and in most superstores. These houses are simple, cheap, and easy to make—you can even make one yourself.

The reed house is constructed from a bunch of reeds of similar size to that required by the bees and 10-15cm in length. These are gathered and blocked off at the back end to make a house. The picture below shows you how this house looks on completion and after the mason bee has been active blocking of the ends of the tubes (*Figure 5*).

Figure 5: Example of Reed mason bee house

Advantages of Reed Houses

Reed houses are very simple to construct and cost very little to make. They are consequently quite desirable to the beekeeper. The reeds are easy to obtain and cut to the correct length. This enables the house to be manufactured and installed quickly. Additionally, with reeds being readily available on the banks of rivers and lakes, the necessary parts are easy to source.

The key advantage of the reed house is its similarity to the natural mason bee habitat. In the wild, the mason bee will look for reeds and holes that are identical to the reed house. The bee will take to this model readily.

Concerns with Reed Houses

These houses are only good for one season. They cannot be taken apart and cleaned and therefore have a limited life for the successful beekeeper. Bees will rarely revisit a hole that has been compromised by the previous generation's debris. Any pests, mites, insects, old cocoons etc. present will lead to the mason bee abandoning the hole and eggs midseason. A build-up of pests and debris over the first two years will prevent the bees from returning to the house altogether. Mason bees are unable to clean out the detritus from a previous season.

Without the ability to clean, the garbage and pests will build up in the nest until the bees will refuse to use them.

We do not recommend this housing for long term bee survival.

Paper Straw Houses

Mason Bee houses that use paper straws are normally to found at garden centres, garden fairs or events, and online retailers. These houses work by the insertion of paper straws into a block of wood, which are then able to be removed at the end of each pollination season (Figure 6). Less often they are strapped together in a group and protected from weather conditions.

The straw house is constructed in the same manner as the reed house. Gather a bunch of suitable sized straws (not plastic) and gather into a bunch. (*Figure 6*). They should be 10-15cm long

Figure 6: Example mason bee paper straws

Advantages of Paper Straw Houses

Paper straw houses are utilised by mason bees since they closely replicate the natural holes they use in the wild. Additionally, the paper straws offer a lower risk of mold in the cells for the bee.

When used within a wood or branch setting, shown in figure 10, below, they offer the closest type of home as experienced by the mason bee. In *figure 10* you can see the loose hole the straw is placed in, this is incorrect. The hole should be tight around the straw to prevent insects and pests climbing into the gap between the straw and the wall.

When maintaining a straw house, you may find that paper straws inserted into holes allow easy access and removal, which means the cocoons can be easily cleaned, using the method outlined in the chapter '*The Beekeeper Calendar, Fall*', and kept inside your home at the end of each season.

Paper straws must be cleaned out and replaced each season. The cocoons will need to be extracted in the fall for this type of house to be viable long term for the following bee generations.

Concerns with Paper Straw Houses

Paper straw houses can get quite expensive over time. New straws will need to be purchased each year. Mason bee, specific straws, can cost as much as $1.50 each and should never be substituted with plastic straws as the dimensions will not be exact. Plastic straws will also retain moisture which increases the temperature in the straw and can rot or cook the cocoons from the inside resulting in non-viable cocoons for the next year.

Pests also invade houses and cannot be cleaned out; they are less prevalent than in reed houses, but the build-up over 2–3 years can result in challenges for the bees laying eggs. It is imperative that the straws are replaced every year and that the hole that the straw is pushed into is harvested of cocoons each fall and cleaned each year to reduce the possibility of pests entering they hole and not the straw.

With proper maintenance the straw tube house can be a good viable form of housing.

Drilled Hole Houses

Drilled hole houses are the closest style to natural holes. They are holes of the bee's preferred length and size drilled into a post, tree, or block.

The drilled hole house is the simplest to construct and is a row of holes drilled into a log or a piece of wood. See the photo below for an example (*Figure 7*).

Figure 7: Example of Drilled hole mason bee house

Advantages of Drilled Hole Houses

We cannot understate the simplicity of drilling a hole and watching for bees. The bees will normally seek out a hole like their natural habitat, most often in a log or tree. Since the drilled hole house is a log, this housing satisfies the bees natural nesting instincts.

Concerns with Drilled Hole Houses

As few as 10-20% of mason bee cocoons are likely to survive the season when laid in holes in the natural environment. This is due to pests or water entering the hole and the inability for the hole to be cleaned. This also applies to drilled hole houses after the first year, as they are just as susceptible to natural dangers.

Although cost effective, these drilled logs are not good for increasing the population of mason bees.

Separable Tray Houses

Separable tray houses are sold under many names but are often referred to as the professional or semi-professional mason bee house. Much thought has been given to mimic the natural habitat of the wild bee, whilst ensuring that the maximum number of cocoons can be brought to maturity. The house is made of a series of trays which form a grid of precisely sized holes for the bee to enter. They are protected by an overhang and can be quickly taken apart to care for the bees at the end of the season.

The trays and mechanism allow for quick and easy separation for cleaning. This facility aids the success rate for bees and the preparation for next year's bumper cocoon crop.

Advantages of Separable Tray Houses

The easy cleaning and safe removal of the cocoons at the necessary time of year ensures that the maximum number of mason bees will survive.

This type of house is the most successful at maintaining a healthy population of mason bees, and a good separable tray house could last several years, if looked after properly.

Concerns with Separable Tray Houses

Separable tray houses are challenging to make, both for companies and individuals. The house may not work in the desired manner if not constructed correctly. Companies will refrain from making these houses in favour of other, simpler styles, therefore they are rarely available in retail 'bog box' stores. You will only find them at specific stores like Long Live Bees and reputable garden centres, plus online stores dedicated to proper mason bee care and management. They are more expensive due to the amount of work that goes into the design and construction. In terms of increased survival of cocoons each year, they pay dividends, and last longer than other forms of bee housing.

These houses also require a little more upkeep—approximately 3–5 hours per year. Most of this time is spent cleaning the house at the end of the year, but even this can be enjoyable as you are playing a very active part in sustaining the mason bee population.

Long Live Bees recommend only using a separable tray house and avoiding all other styles where possible. We neither sell nor produce any other model of mason bee house.

Chapter 5

Make Your Own Mason Bee House

Commercial companies have noticed the growing interest in mason bees in the past few years and have hooked onto the idea of selling their own mason bee houses in the form of fixed reeds or wooden hole models of house. They typically carry names such as 'bug house' or 'bee house'. Whilst attractive for humans to look at they are usually of cheap construction and built for profit rather than a desire to aid the pollinator. The fixed nature of the nesting holes does not allow for the cleaning of the compartments, resulting in an inefficient house. The population of parasites also increases, and further limits the mason bee's ability to nest. These model of house do more harm to the bee than good.

Typically, the dangers go unnoticed because the mason bees will still use the bee house provided in the first season. After hatching, they need somewhere to lay their eggs and call home, and the familiarity of the location where there were hatched draws them back repeatedly. Inside the housing, however, the bees' eggs, larvae, and pupae are probably dying at a much higher rate than when the house was first installed. If the same house is left out for several years, it might do more to increase the population of pests than mason bees.

Instead of relying on a company's creation that may or may not be good for the bees, you can try your own hand at building one (or more) of the style of house yourself using our simple steps.

Important Note: Suitable Nesting Box Placement

Where you place your mason bee house is as important as the house you build. Let us examine the location before considering how we build a house.

The location must be dry, about 1–1.5 m (4–5 feet) from the ground and south-facing to gain maximum sun. The ideal location for your bee house is on a larger building, tree, house, or garden shed wall. Mason bees seek out the security of being close to a large object, and they expect to locate more holes around the same area.

Ensure that flowers and/or fruit trees are available within 60 m (200 feet) of the nest. Mason bees will travel up to 90 m (300 feet) for pollen, but they like the food source to be as close as possible to their nest. See *Chapter 9* for a list of appropriate plants.

The nesting house, being made of wood, is very susceptible to the effects of rain and should have a covering roof that protects the nest from drips down the front and sides. Holes should be tilted very slightly downward towards the front. This will reduce the possibility of rainwater entering and harming the nest and cocoons.

Do not place the house on a movable object or anything that moves in the wind. Bees dislike movement in their nest, and they will move onto another location if the nest moves too much.

Female mason bees require mud for the walls they build to protect their eggs, so it's important to have open clay-based soil (without grass or bark covering) near the nest. Do not keep mud available directly under the nest, since the bees are very weak when they first leave hibernation, and they could fall off the nest into the mud.

If you wish to help the bee you can dig a hole approximately 2-3 inches deep in an area of your garden. Keep the sides of the hole moist but not too wet. In the mornings the bee will use the sides near the top of the hole to collet mud. As the mud dries, they will venture further down the sides. Make sure there is not a puddle of water at the bottom. Place some stones at the bottom of the hole for the bee to stand on.

How to Make a Reed House

You will need:

- 15–30 reeds, with an opening of approximately 8 mm (5/16th inch) (Figure 8)
- String or twine
- An overhang to secure to the top of the reed house
- A suitable location for your mason bee house

Procedure:

1. Gather the reeds from either a garden centre, or along a river or creek.

    o Ensure that your reeds are firm, fully dried, and free of leaves before continuing.

2. Cut your reeds into 10–20 cm (4–8 inch) lengths, just below the "knee," or bump in the reed. Ensure that there are no other bumps along the shaft.

3. Tie your reeds together with string or twine, where all the "knee" ends are on the same side. This end will be at the back of the house.

4. Add an overhanging roof to protect the reeds from the rain.

5. Hang your bee house in a suitable location.

Maintenance:

At the start of each season (middle of March), remove some of the bundle of reeds and place them somewhere safe, a short distance from the main house pack. Add a selection of new tubes to the main bundle and place the new house back into position. If you do this every year, the bees will be tempted to fill up the new tubes you added to the bundle. You can discard the removed tubes when the bees in the tubes have hatched.

Over the course of 3 years, you can replace all the tubes and start again!

Figure 8: Reed Mason Bee House

How to Make a Paper Straw House

Method 1: Bundled Straws
You will need:

- 15-20 strong paper straws, with an opening of approximately 8 mm (5/16th inch) (*Figure 9*)
- DO NOT use plastic straws, as they promote rotting in cocoons due to overheating and damp.

- String or twine
- A suitable location for your mason bee house

Procedure:

1. Cut your straws into 10–20 cm (4–8 inch) lengths.

2. Squeeze one end of the all the straws shut so that no light may enter.

3. Tie your straws together with string or twine, with all the closed ends on the same side.

4. Place the straws into a wooden box, with the closed ends toward the back of the box.

5. Hang your bee house in a suitable location.

Figure 9: Example straws for mason bee house

Method 2: Straws-in-Holes

You will need:

- 15-20 strong paper straws, with an opening of approximately 8 mm (5/16th inch) (Figure ??)
- DO NOT use plastic straws, as they promote rotting in cocoons.
- A block of wood
- A drill
- A suitable location for your mason bee house

Procedure:

1. Cut your straws into 10–20 cm (4–8 inch) lengths.

2. Measure the diameter of the outer edge of one straw.

3. Drill a hole into the block of wood with the same diameter as your straw's outer edge.
   o Ensure that there are no gaps between the edge of the straw and the drilled hole to minimize pest infestations.

   o Do not drill through the back of the wooden block.

4. Insert your straw into the hole.

5. Repeat steps 2–4 for all your straws.

6. Hang your bee house in a suitable location.

This method can be more work, but it is more successful in allowing the eggs to fully mature. Figure 10 shows how NOT to make a paper straw house, these are much too loose in the hole.

Figure 10: Straws in mason bee house

Maintenance:

At the end of the season, bring the straws inside and place them somewhere cool (such as a garage or shed). In October or November, open the straws carefully either by unravelling or soaking in tepid water first for a few minutes and carefully remove the healthy cocoons. Dispose of any dirt etc. along with the straws.

Follow the steps provided in *Chapter 7:* for more details on how to clean the house. Remember that you must buy new straws at the start of each season.

How to make a Drilled Hole House

You will need:

- A drill, 8 mm (5/16th inch) in diameter
- A suitable surface to drill into, at least 20 cm (8 inches) deep

- Wood is the best choice, but you may also use branches or tree trunks. If using a tree trunk do not harm the tree by putting an excessive number of holes in the trunk
- A suitable location for your mason bee house
- You may also choose to drill directly into the suitable location

Procedure:

1. Choose the piece of wood, tree, log etc. to drill your holes into.

2. Drill holes 10–20 cm (4–8 inch) deep.
   o The holes should be completely level or point very slightly down.

   o Do not drill through the back of the log.

3. Hang your bee house in a suitable location.

Figure 11: Mason bee capping a drill in a tree log

Maintenance:

Sadly, there is no safe way to maintain this type of house. The simplest and safest way to maintain the house is to leave it alone.

DO NOT be tempted to drill out the holes nor open the house, as either method may kill many bees. The bees will rarely use the same hole for more than two seasons, so this house quickly becomes obsolete. Additionally, fewer only 10 to 20% of eggs laid in these houses are likely to mature and survive.

We recommend using a different style of bee house for more successful results.

How to Make a Separable Tray House

These model of house is the hardest to produce and therefore is generally not available at major outlet stores. There are also, due their complexity, challenging to make and, necessarily, more expensive from specialist stores. They are also the most successful for keeping mason bees and have the greatest success rate year on year.

Method 1: Drill

You will need:

- A drill, 8 mm (5/16th inch) in diameter
- 5–6 pieces of wood, 15 cm (6 inches) long, 10-15cm (4–6 inches) wide and 1.25 cm (0.5 inches) deep
- A bar of 15 cm (6 inch) length with a wing nut
- A suitable location for your mason bee house

Procedure:

1. Clamp the pieces of wood tightly together with the joins running vertically.

2. Drill straight down into the line where two pieces of wood meet, to a maximum depth of 20 cm (8 inches; see Figure 12, below).

    o The drilled hole should create a half-moon on each side of the wood.

    o Do not drill through the back of the block.

3. Drill through the stack of trays, avoiding any channels (drills) and put the bar through one side, securing with the wing nut on the other. If the trays slide, then it may be necessary to add another bar ten centimeter away (4 inch).

Figure 12: Example Separate tray mason bee house (assembled)

Method 2: Router

You will need:

- 6-8 pieces of wood, 10–20 cm (4–8 inches) wide, 1.25 cm (0.5 inches) thick, and 20 cm (8 inches) long
- A router table
- A bar of 15 cm (6 inch) length with a wing nut
- A suitable location for your mason bee house

Procedure:

1. Set your router table to a depth of 4 mm with a round head or square head bit of 8 mm.

2. Set the fence to 5 mm away from the back of the bit.

3. Make a channel along the complete distance of the board.

4. Clean the channel.

5. Move the fence back 23 mm.

    o This distance is the width of the router head (8 mm) plus 15 mm.

6. Repeat steps 2–5 until you have gone across the width of the board.

7. Cut the board into 15 cm (6 inch) lengths and stack them together.

    o Ensure that the channels are correctly aligned.

8. Drill vertically through the stack of trays, avoiding any channels, and put the bar through one side, securing with the wing nut on the other (Figure 13).

- If the trays slide, you may need to add another bar ten centimeter (4 inches) away.

9. Add a board across the back to protect the rear of the house.
   - Ensure that the board does not allow any light into the hole.

Figure 13: Example securing bar through trays – fixed by butterfly nut

Method 3: Table Saw

You will need:

- A piece of wood, 10–15 cm (4–6 inches) wide, 2.5 cm (1 inch) thick, and over 15 cm (6 inches) long
- A table saw set up with a 8mm dado blade
- A bar of 15 cm (6 inch) length with a wing nut
- A suitable location for your mason bee house

Procedure:

1. Set the saw depth to 8mm and run the wood along the fence, 5 mm from the edge.
2. Repeat very close to the last cut to form a hole 8 mm deep, across the full length of the board.
3. Move the wood across 10–15 mm and repeat 2. above, until you have crossed the whole board.
4. Cut the board into 13–15 cm (5–6 inch) lengths and stack them together.
    o The holes will be square, but this does not scare away the bees if the holes are the correct dimensions.
5. Drill vertically through the stack of trays, avoiding any channels, and put the bar through one side, securing with the wing nut on the other.
    o If the trays slide, you may need to add another bar ten centimeter (4 inches) away.
6. Add a board across the back to protect the rear of the house.
    o Ensure that the board does not allow any light into the hole.

Maintenance for a separable tray house is in Chapter 6: *The Beekeeper Calendar*.

*NOTE: From this point in the book onwards, we will only discuss the **separable tray house** as a means of housing your bees.*

Long Live Bees has a strong preference for this housing for the following reasons:

- This style is the most successful at increasing bee populations.

- It is easy to clean and restore each year.

- The house can survive for many seasons due to its ability to come apart for cleaning.

- It's maintenance can provide hours of fun for family and friends.

Chapter 6

The Beekeeper Calendar

Chapter 6 will describe the annual actions needed by the mason beekeeper, with approximate timing and schedule. The chapter is broken into the four seasons of the year. There may be a slight overlap in some areas, depending on when the bees hatch and when the spring commences for plants and trees.

Each section includes tasks that need to be performed and an estimate of timing. We have not considered the many happy hours of time you will spend watching your bees at work.

Spring

Spring is the time of activity for the mason beekeeper; we are checking our bee cocoons, siting our houses, and monitoring weather and plant development.

Activity: Siting Your Mason Bee House (March-April)

Time spent: 15 minutes.

The first task is to find a suitable site for the mason bee house. The house will need to be in a position that is:

- 4–7ft above the ground for optimal viewing. We have heard of separable bee houses successfully placed on balconies on the third floor, however it is unlikely that mason bees would fly any higher.

- In a south-facing position (into the sun) if possible. It is not disastrous if the house is not faced towards the sun, but it benefits the bees by helping them warm up quicker in the early morning.

- In an area protected from the elements. The Bees do not enjoy rain and will not use a nest that is wet or damp. Placing the house under an eave, tree branch, or some other protection helps the cocoon survival rate. Houses exposed to the elements tend to soak up water over the course of the spring and summer, causing damp and mold to the innermost cocoons, which do not survive.

If possible, place the house so that the bees have access to mud, not over grass. They need mud to build their walls between the eggs. If water is close by, the bees will be more productive. Water mixed with soil will speed their wall building.

Activity: Introducing the cocoons to the housing

Time spent: 30 minutes.

Note: If you are purchasing an initial cohort of cocoons for a 54-hole house, 25 is a good number to start with. You can expect these to at least have doubled by the end of the season.

Putting up a mason bee house and waiting for native bees to inhabit the holes can be hit and miss. If you know that there is already a healthy population of native bees in your garden then fine, however many of us do not have existing native mason bees in abundance, if at all. Purchasing a minimum of 25 cocoons (obtainable from garden centres or companies online) will give the area a great start from which to develop a thriving population.

You will know that your housing will have guaranteed occupants if you hatch your cocoons near to the housing.

The following is the correct way to introduce your new pack of cocoons to the house: -

The mason bee is an early riser in the season. In the Western United States and Canada, it will emerge from its cocoon towards the end of spring (March-April). However, timing may differ elsewhere in the world. You will know it is time to release your bees when:

- It is mid-March, at the earliest. Do not be tempted to put out the cocoons too early, they will disappear on exit, or die in the cocoon.
- You have at least three consecutive days where the temperature will be above 15 °C (60 °F).
- It does not rain within those three consecutive days. The bees will not emerge into rain unless it is late in the season.
- Flowers, fruit trees, and other plants have begun blooming, and at least 25% of flowers are open.
- It is not beyond the end of April. Typically, the 15th–25th of April is the latest hatching date. If your cocoons remain in the fridge beyond this date, they will begin to hatch in their container. Nature dictates they will hatch towards the end of April, even if it is still cold.

After purchasing your new set of cocoons for your condominium, you will typically keep them in the fridge (or a cold area in the house/shed/garage) until the outside temperatures are suitable for release. In the wild the bees sense the change of temperature and start to wake up, sometimes disastrously if there is a subsequent frost or cold spell. Bees can take cold weather, but not freezing temperatures once they have hatched. By engineering the optimum time for release, we are increasing the chances of life after hatching.

When you feel the time is right to release your bees, place your cocoons in a small box or bottle with a hole in one side, 8 mm ($5/16^{th}$ inch) in diameter. The cocoons should not sit on top of each other or be more than two deep; there should be enough room for several bees to freely move around when they hatch. For example, a matchbox would hold around 25 bees comfortably.

Secure the box containing the cocoons on or close to the bee house to prevent it moving in the wind. Ensure that there is an opening in the box for the newly hatched bees to emerge. Protect it from the weather as much as you can but allow it to get sunshine if possible. The bees will start to emerge during the next few days.

Your task for this part of the season is complete, but the bees' work is just beginning. Enjoy watching them emerge from the box, investigate a new hole, rush from plant to plant, and zoom in and out of their nest. Throughout the spring, you can watch out for these things to enhance your beekeeping experience:

1. The first bees to emerge will be the males. You can identify them by the white tufts of hair on their heads. They are also smaller than the females.

2. Look for the pollen on the female as she returns to the nest. If she has a clean abdomen, she will be bringing back mud to build the walls between the cells in the tunnel.

3. Watch the female as she adds her closing mud plug. She will go around the hole's opening as she works to close the egg chamber and the tunnel.

4. At night or in the early morning, use a covered flashlight to see the bees resting in the front of their holes. Their little eyes will be looking right at you!

5. During this time, pay attention to which plants your bees like to frequent. Make a note, to plant more of these the next year, to ensure that your next season's bees will be even happier.

6. You will be amazed at the energy and the frenetic flying in and out of the holes all day. Activity commences once the bees have woken in the morning, they will appear at the entrance of their hole for a few minutes to warm up before flying off.

7. Sometimes the bee flies back into the wrong hole. Watch how she gets chased out by the occupant, or suddenly realises she isn't home after all!

8. Sometimes a bee may land on you or circle around you. Do not be afraid, they will not sting or be aggressive. They are very gentle creatures and will take off in their own time.

9. Don't be too disappointed if some cocoons don't hatch at all after two weeks. Some just don't make it.

10. Not all newly hatched bees will use the housing, no matter how attractive it is. They are after all wild creatures and they will make their own mind up where to make their home.

Summer

Throughout April and early May, you can enjoy watching your mason bees finalise their work. The mason bee doesn't live very long as an adult; the males will live 1–2 weeks, and the females 4–6 weeks. In this short period, the female must lay her eggs and collect enough pollen to feed her brood.

Once summer arrives, the mason bee's work is complete. You should consider taking down the house for protection during August, but if you choose to leave out a little longer, you may also be pleasantly surprised to see other visitors to your bee house. Leafcutter bees which are a native early summer solitary bee may wish to make the house their home, and although they prefer smaller holes, they will happily work with the mason bee's 8 mm holes.

The mason beekeeper can keep themselves occupied by enhancing the garden for other pollinators and insects. The needs of other pollinators are similar to that of the mason bee; they require pollen, water, and a place to nest safely. We recommend that you choose an area of your garden to grow freely with wildflowers and plants. The area must be one that you do not frequent very often, is not visited by children or pets, and has no pesticides used near to it. In no time at all, you will see beetles, butterflies, and other creatures making this area their home.

Remember to also plan your next year's garden during this time. It may be a little early to plant any new trees or flowers, however you can plan and prepare for the following year.

See *Chapter 9* for a list of suggested plants for your pollinator-friendly garden.

Activity: Taking Down Your Mason Bee House (August)

Time spent: 15 minutes.

If you have a separable or a straw house, then this next task is essential for the maximum survival of your cocoons. If you have the reed or drilled version of the mason bee house then it is recommended, if possible, that you also undertake this task.

Task: Take down the mason bee house from where you had placed it. Do not shake or drop the house, remember, there are living creatures inside and they do not take kindly to rough handling.

If you have a Long Live Bees BeeSafe bag, (close weave recycled net bag), then place the house inside and pull the drawstring tight. The net bag will prevent unwelcome insects and bugs entering and nesting in the house throughout the winter.

Identify a location in a garage or shed that will not be disturbed and place your mason bee house on its back, holes facing up somewhere where it will not be disturbed.

When placing your house somewhere safe for the winter you will need to ensure that there is no entrance to the nest from any direction, so fold the opening of the net bag under the house.

When the mason bee lays eggs, it collects the pollen first and then lays the egg on top of the pollen. To ensure that the bee egg maximises its contact with the pollen we place the bee house on its back so that the egg rolls or falls into the pollen and does not have to climb the chamber to reach its food.

You can now leave the housing alone, however, periodically check the bag for intruders. Sometimes insect pests can enter the housing before you take it down, then they exit and find themselves in the net bag. Dispose of any earwigs etc. and kill any small flies/tiny wasps you may find in the bag. These can be houdini flies and monodontomerous wasps. They enter the house and lay their eggs in the cocoons.

Fall

Fall is the more time-consuming period for a mason beekeeper, as you will need to clean your bee house, harvest, and inspect your bees, and get rid of any pests which may be in there.

Activity: Cleaning and Harvesting the Cocoons (October/November)

Time spent: 1 hour.

This is when the fun starts in your mason beekeeping. You will soon know how many bees you are taking into next spring. This may well be your first-generation offspring.

Your mason bee house will look something like the picture in figure 14, below. There will be capped off holes (if you are lucky) and the occasional blank hole. Do not underestimate the importance of these blank holes, there is a possibility that they are part filled. The mason bee may have died before completing the filling of the drill, with the result that there are some females laying at the back of the hole.

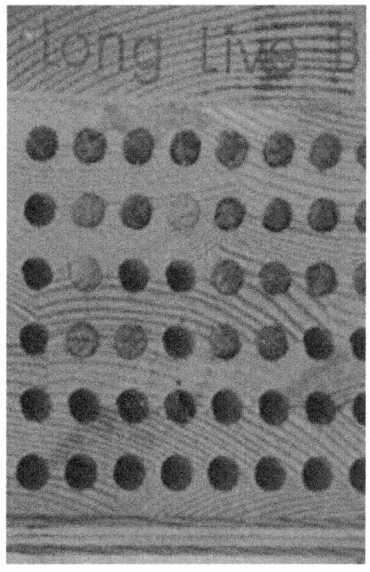

Figure 14: Mason bee house at end of the season

Before you open the separable tray house, find a location where there is water and somewhere to wash the trays without splashing everywhere. A sink and table can be used inside, though some people prefer outside. We find it helps to be near a sink for washing and rinsing.

Figure 15: Tools ready for cleaning separable mason bee house

You will need (Figure 15):

- a large bowl of lukewarm water
- a colander or old sieve
- newspaper
- kitchen roll
- an old towel
- screwdriver
- old toothbrush or scrubbing brush

Procedure:

1. Open the separable tray house by removing the wing screws or nut on the bottom. Try not to disturb the trays when you remove the bolts.

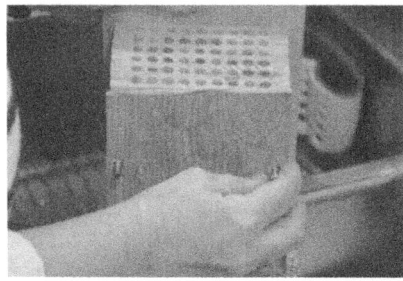

Figure 16: Unscrewing the condo to separate trays

2. Slowly remove the trays. Be extra careful because bees and debris may fall off the drills (the channels the bees are laid in). Lay some white paper underneath the bee house so that you can see what is falling off.

The drills will not be exclusively filled with neatly arranged cocoons; there will also be dirt, detritus, and maybe some unwanted visitors such as grubs, maggots, and insects.

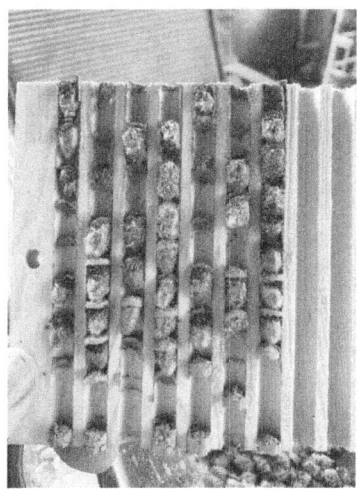

Figure 17: A typical view inside a tray from the mason bee house

What you may find upon opening your separable tray house:

- Bee cocoons: female at the back, male at the front.
- Bee meconium (poop): small black flecks or strands.
- Mud plugs between each cocoon.
- Pollen in the place of where a cocoon should be. This would mean the egg did not mature, which can happen if the pollen is too wet or sticky.
- Pests: carpet beetles, earwigs, and/or pollen mites. Dispose of any you find. Mites will be washed off when you clean the cocoons.

- Chalkbrood: a fungal disease which kills the larva when they ingest it. It is grey/white in colour. If found on the surface of the cocoons, the bees inside should still be alive, however the cocoons should be disinfected to prevent passing it onto bees when they hatch. If you find chalkbrood on any cocoons, separate them from cocoons without chalkbrood.
- Checkered flower beetle larvae: these are quite large and white. Discard immediately.

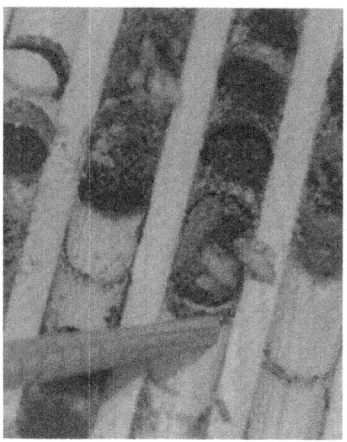

Figure 18: Houdini maggots, close-up

- Houdini fly maggots (kleptoparasites): found in clusters between cocoons. The houdini fly waits around outside bee nests in the spring waiting for an opportune moment to fly inside and lay its eggs in a pollen deposit. When the fly eggs hatch, the fly larvae eat the pollen and the bee egg. The following spring, they hatch at the same time as the mason bee and begin the cycle again. The Houdini fly is an invasive species which has been a growing issue for mason bees in the past few years

WHAT CAN WE DO? All we can do to prevent this pest from laying its eggs in the condos is to stay watchful outside the bee house. If you see a little fly hanging around the bee house, squish it. You don't need to camp out but be extra vigilant during the time that the bees are active.

- Using the end of a screwdriver, carefully scrape the cocoons into the bowl of lukewarm water. Check both sides of the trays. Keep going until you have done them all.

Figure 19: Scrape out and wash

3. Wash the cocoons thoroughly, then drain through a colander.

DO NOT Leave the cocoons in the water for longer than a few minutes. The water will weaken the tough structure of the cocoon and the bees will not withstand winter storage.

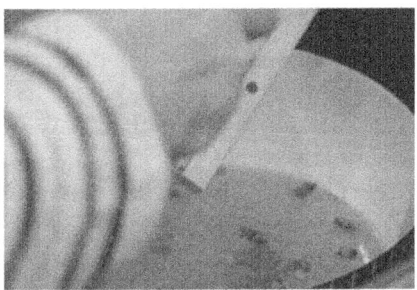

Figure 20: Do not waterlog the cocoons

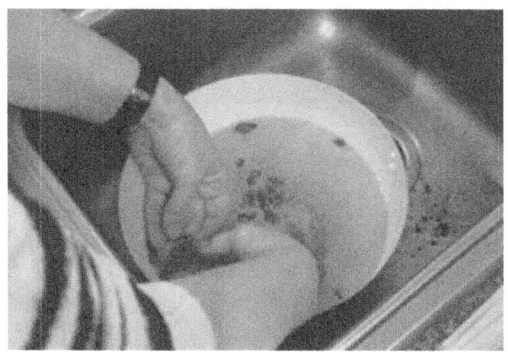

Figure 21: Wash and repeat

4. Repeat step 2 until there is no dirt left, just cocoons and clean water.

Figure 22: Rinse

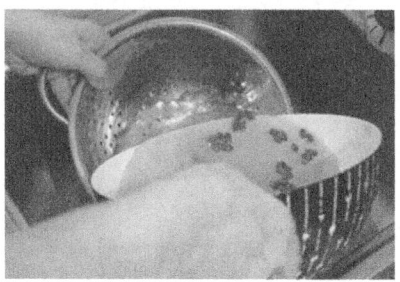

Figure 23: And rinse again

Lay down an old towel and lay paper towel on top of it. Tip the cocoons onto the paper towel and tap the tops dry with more paper. Transfer the cocoons to a dry kitchen towel.

5. Inspect the cocoons for the sex of each cell (Figure 24).

Figure 24: Sexing the cocoons

The larger cocoons are females, and the smaller ones are males. Non-viable cocoons may be small, squishy, wrinkly, and paler in colour; they may also sink in the water bath, be C-shaped, or have holes in them. Destroy any non-viable cocoons. Keep any you are not sure of separate from the healthy cocoons.

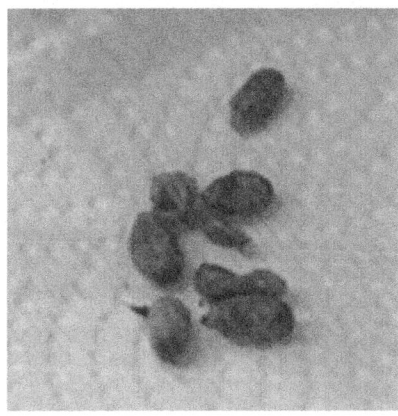

Figure 25: Questionable cocoons

6. Leave the cocoons to dry for an hour, then transfer to a plastic container. Make sure the lid is pierced with a couple of ventilation holes. At this point, you may notice the cocoons have a distinct odour; this is normal.

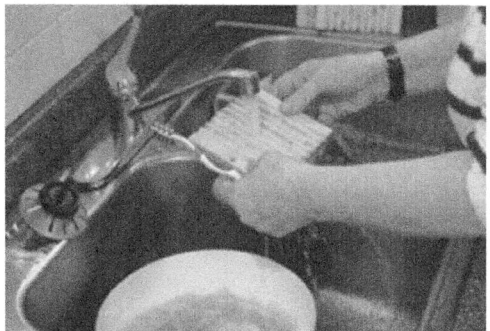

Figure 26: Disinfecting cocoons and trays

7. If you see chalkbrood or are unsure of the cleanliness of your cocoons, you may want to disinfect them. Disinfect by washing the cocoons for several seconds (10-30) in two litres of water to a tablespoon of bleach. Make sure to thoroughly rinse and dry. You can also disinfect if you find mold on the cocoons whilst storing in the fridge over the winter.

Figure 27: Cleaning the condo

Cleaning Your Separable Tray House

Once the job of washing the cocoons is done, you can turn your attention to the separable tray house itself. Proper cleaning is essential to provide your bees with a sanitized home next spring.

8. Using an old toothbrush, scrub the housing and the trays with warm water and dish soap. Dispose of anything remaining in the drills. Don't be concerned if you see staining on the trays.

9. Rinse the trays and leave to dry.

10. Place the trays in the microwave two at a time and zap on full power for 30 seconds to ensure that no mites are still alive, and the trays are sanitary.

DO NOT microwave the main housing with any metal, the bolts or screws in place. This will damage the microwave.

11. Reassemble the trays and screw together.

This will prevent any warping of the wood resulting from washing. Leave in a dry place for a couple of days to ensure it is thoroughly dry.

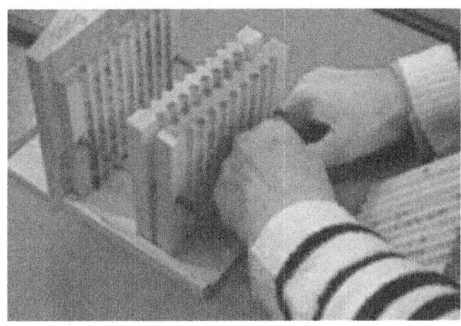

Figure 28: Dry and reassemble the house

Your bees and housing are once again ready for next spring.

Storing Your Cocoons:

The cocoons need to be kept between 2–4 °C (36–39 °F) with 60–70% humidity. The best way to achieve these conditions is by putting your bee cocoons in a manual defrost refrigerator and checking them regularly to ensure the conditions are still ideal.

If you do not have a manual defrost fridge then there are options. A cold area of the shed or garage being one, or they can be placed in a modern frost-free fridge if precautions are taken.

If you don't have access to a manual defrost type of refrigerator (for example, you only have a frost-free refrigerator), will need to regularly introduce water to the refrigerator using one of the following methods:

1. Use a bee humidifier. Put the bee cocoons in one side of the humidifier and water in the other, then put the humidifier in the fridge. If you do not own a bee humidifier then a plastic tub with small holes punched into the top and a small bowl of water in one corner will suffice.

2. Store the cocoons in a container with a couple of ventilation holes in the top and place an open container of water close to the bees. In very dry fridges, place a damp paper towel or a lettuce leaf on a jar lid in the container with the cocoons. The jar lid will prevent the cocoons from touching the water, which reduces the possibility of mold. Replace the damp paper towel or lettuce leaf every week. Make sure to label your container so that no one sprinkles the cocoons on their salad!

Figure 29: Mason bees ready for the winter

DO NOT STORE COCOONS IN ANY TYPE OF FREEZER.

If you don't have access to a refrigerator, you can store your cocoons outside in a shed or garage—however, this should be a last resort. You won't be able to regulate the temperature or humidity with this method, and prolonged freezing weather can be detrimental to bees. The bees may also emerge earlier if there are warm spells. If you choose this method, cocoons should be placed in a cleaned and air-dried cardboard box with a layer of toilet paper. The cardboard box should be placed inside a metal box, such as a coffee can, to prevent predators from eating your cocoons. Puncture holes into the metal container for ventilation. Clearly label the container.

In nature, mason bees within their cocoons can withstand a couple of weeks of below freezing temperatures, although they will not live if weather is extreme for prolonged periods. Mason bees need normal cold winter temperatures for 90–150 days to emerge successfully.

Mold

Mold grows on the cocoons if they are stored in wet or damp conditions and is particularly vigorous if pollen is left on the cocoon's surface. Sometimes, depending on what is also in the fridge, humidity can rise and mold results.

A well-ventilated container should prevent mold growth, but if you see any on the surface of the cocoons, remove by washing the cocoons in two litres of water and one tablespoon of bleach. Dry thoroughly before replacing in the container. You may have to repeat this if your fridge conditions are not ideal.

Winter

There are no significant actions for the mason beekeeper during the winter months. The cocoons are stored safely, and the bee house is ready for the next season. From November through to early March, the tasks are small and quick to perform.

Examine the cocoons once a week in the fridge to ensure that they have sufficient moisture in the air and that no mold is growing.

If you have decided to place the bees in a frost-free fridge then it is essential that you ensure some moisture is in the vicinity of the cocoons. Do not allow the cocoons to get wet but ensure the air around them has some humidity. This can be done by placing a lettuce leaf of two in the container with the cocoons. Ensure you change the lettuce leaf every week and wash the cocoons in a bleach solution of one tablespoon of bleach to one cup of water if they develop mold.

Other than that, you can only anticipate the next season and dream about your garden growing under the pollination of your mason bees!

Chapter 7

Cleaning a Paper Straw House

Although we most highly recommend using a separable tray house for your mason bees, a paper straw house is a good alternative. Like the separable tray house, the paper straw house can also be cleaned and reused for years to come with the following steps.

You will need:

- A bowl of cool water
- New, clean paper straws (the same number as you are removing from the house)
- An empty storage tub for the cocoons when removed
- Straw cleaning brush

Procedure:

1. Carefully remove the straws. Take care not to squeeze the tube as you may damage the cocoons inside.

    o It may be hard to remove some straws as they will have settled into the holes. If possible, check the rear of the tube for any mud or twigs preventing its removal. Avoid forcing the straw; instead, use as much care as you can to ensure the survival of as many cocoons as possible.

2. Set the straws to one side while you examine the house for damage. Repair as necessary.

The cocoons are at rest within the straws. If you hold the straw up to the light, you will see the cocoons lined up, side by side. Treat the straws carefully, as we do not want to harm the cocoons.

3. Carefully unwrap the straw from one end. This will be easy if you are using the correct mason bee straws. If you are using cheap or plastic straws this technique will not work.

 Do not be tempted to open the straw if you have straws that will not unwrap. It is recommended that you leave the cocoons inside the straw and place them in a safe location without opening. In the spring you can place the straws outside near the new home and allow any bees that can escape to use the new environment. If the straws will not unwrap, soak them in tepid water for a minute which will make the task easier. However, do not allow the straws to rest too long in water or you may weaken the structure of the cocoon.

4. Separate the cocoons from the mud and other pests.

From this point, follow the instructions from Chapter 6 *Fall*, steps 4-7. Cleaning Your Separable House

5. On step 5, cleaning the mason bee house you will use the straw cleaning brush to push down into each drill (hole).

6. If you have no metal, nails, pins, staples etc. in the house then you can add extra cleaning by placing the wooden trays in the microwave for 30 seconds. **Do not place in microwave machine if any metal is present, it will damage the microwave.**

Chapter 8

Pests and Diseases

As mason beekeepers, we should do what we can to keep the bees and cocoons healthy and safe. But before we can protect, we must first learn the dangers.

Caring for mason bees in a natural environment means that predators and pests are bound to be present. The sweet smell of pollen draws many pests in, and once the holes are infested, the cocoons inside are in danger.

Wild mason bees do not often make their nesting holes very close to one another unless there is no suitable alternative, which ensures that the infestation of one nest won't spread easily to any others. However man-made bee houses have holes in close proximity, and the diseases and pests of one hole can quickly spread to others. Long Live Bees recommend bee houses that can be taken apart and thoroughly cleaned—such as separable tray houses (see Chapter 4, Separable Tray Houses)—to better control the spread of infestations.

Inevitably, no matter how careful you are, you will encounter diseases and pests in your bee house. However, with some background knowledge and a keen eye, you may be able to stop them before they cause havoc and the destruction of your cocoons.

General Garden Pests

Birds

Foraging birds may sit on the roofs of bee houses and try to peck at filled nesting holes. If you have bird nests on or around your property, the birds may try swooping and catching bees in flight. Swallows are particularly partial to this activity, and woodpeckers can peck for larvae and cocoons in the housing. The bees are especially vulnerable in the early morning when they bask in the sun to warm up enough to fly.

ACTION: Loosely tack a wire netting with 3/4" openings around the housing. Leave 3" between the netting and the nesting holes to allow the bees free movement. Do not site bird nesting boxes near to the housing.

Ants

Ants are attracted to the smell of pollen, bee cocoons, and larvae, all of which have a distinct odor. One or two ants are no problem, but the uncommon occurrence of a colony invading the nesting holes can result in the bees abandoning the nest.

ACTION: Wrap a sticky tree band (we recommend Tanglefoot) or Vaseline around the base of the post or wall that holds the bee house. The band will catch any ants and prevent them from crossing the barrier.

Earwigs

Earwigs are attracted to the pollen, eggs, and larvae. They are very skilled at getting into the holes and eating larvae as they develop.

ACTION: Since earwigs like moist, damp places, distract them from the bee house by rolling up a dampened newspaper, tying it with string or an elastic band, and hanging it near (but not too close) to the bee house. The newspaper will draw the earwigs away from the holes. Replace or re-wet the newspaper weekly.

It also helps to keep the bee housing in a dry area of the garden.

Paper Wasps and Social Hornets

Paper wasps and social hornets will not attack your bee housing or eat the bees, but they may attach their nests to the underside of the housing or any nearby cavities. Their proximity to the bee house could cause a huge nuisance to you, rather than doing any damage to the bees.

ACTION: If you have a paper wasp infestation, wait until late evening—when the wasps are settled—and spray the paper wasp nest with a jet hose. Gently remove it by scraping the wasp nest away. Then fill any leftover spaces with twigs and wadded paper to deter them from re-nesting. NOTE: Do not use pesticides at any point, as this will kill your bees.

If you have a social hornet infestation (such as yellowjackets) DO NOT remove the nest yourself. Instead, call a professional as soon as possible.

Pests from Spring to Fall

Bee larvae develop from spring to fall, which attracts several pests. They are difficult to keep out of bee housing, but careful management while storing and cleaning your house can limit the spread from one year to the next.

Houdini Fly

These small grey flies with red eyes hang around mason bee nesting places. They enter the holes and eat the pollen loaf meant for the bee larvae, which subsequentially dies without its nutrients. The houdini flies then lay their eggs in the holes which emerge as adults in the spring. When cleaning the bee house in the fall, you may see white or pale-yellow maggots in the cavity where a bee cocoon should be.

ACTION: When you clean and harvest bee cocoons in the fall, remove and kill any fly maggots. Place the bee house in a protective net storage bag (we recommend our Bee Safe bag) and tie at the end, then store in an unheated garage or shed. If your bee housing does not come apart for cleaning, keep it in the protective net storage bag until spring and kill any adult flies that emerge.

Monodontomerus

Monodontomerus (also known as mono) are gnat-sized parasitic wasps. They have long black ovipositors (egg layers), which they use to penetrate through cracks in mason bee mud walls, nesting tubes, or other nesting materials and inject their eggs. The mason bee larva constructs it's cocoon and consequently envelopes the mono larva, which then eats the bee from the inside. You can identify a mono infestation by the hole the adult wasp makes in the cocoon as it chews its way out.

ACTION: If your bee cocoons do not hatch within a week of release, they could be infested by mono wasps and should be destroyed. You can't do much to prevent infestation whilst the mason bees are active, however when the season is finished, take the housing down in July/August and place in a protective net storage bag. After a week, check the bag. Any adult mono wasps that have emerged will be trapped in the bag and can be killed. Store the house in the protective net storage bag to prevent further infestation.

Sapgid Wasp

Sapgid wasps, or sapgya, are about 1/3 inch long. They look similar to hornets and yellow-jackets, as they sometimes have yellow spots and a maroon band. The female finds a mason bee hole and inserts her egg into the mud cap. The wasp egg hatches in 1–2 days, then eats the bee egg and the pollen loaf. It spins its own cocoon and overwinters alongside the other mason bee cocoons in the hole and emerges at the same time as the mason bees.

ACTION: If you see any sapgya wasps flying zig zag outside your mason bee housing, spray them with a fine mist of water to stun them and destroy them immediately.

Pests During the Fall

You may encounter the following pests whilst harvesting cocoons and cleaning your bee housing.

Pollen Mites

Pollen mites are microscopic mites that live on flower pollen. They are often inadvertently picked up by bees and taken back to the nesting holes, where if in large quantities the mites eat the pollen loaf and starve the mason bee larvae. The mites overwinter in the nesting holes, and when healthy adult bees leave the holes in the following spring, they walk through the chambers infected with pollen mites and spread the mites to the new holes. You will know you have an infestation when you open the bee housing to clean and spot a yellow or orange mass of loosely packed mite feces where a bee cocoon should be.

ACTION: Pollen mites easily spread, so do not reuse housing materials. You may reuse wooden trays for separable tray houses if cleaned thoroughly (see Chapter X). When harvesting bee cocoons in the fall, wash all cocoons twice in a bleach solution (1 gallon of water and 1 teaspoon of household bleach). Dry the cocoons on an old towel to reduce chance of rot.

Chalkbrood

Chalkbrood is a fungal infection that mason bees pick up from flowers. The bees then bring the chalkbrood back to their nesting holes where it is ingested by bee larvae. The infection kills the larvae, which then becomes a mass of chalkbrood spores. You can identify a chalkbrood infection as the dead larvae will be chalky, break apart easily, and curled into a "C" shape. The dead larvae may be brown, gray, charcoal, or salmon in color with a black, powdery finish. If the dead larvae are left in the nesting hole, healthy bees can brush past infected chambers and further the spread.

ACTION: In the fall, harvest and clean your mason bee housing and dispose of any chalk brood cadavers. Do not allow any healthy cocoons to touch them. Wash the healthy cocoons in a bleach solution (1 gallon of water with 1 teaspoon of household bleach), then rinse and dry thoroughly. Scrub the housing trays with soapy water and dry, before reassembling and storing it in a protective net storage bag for the next spring.

Meal Moths, Carpet Beetles and Ptinus Beetles

These three insects are not deterred by the mud walls that mason bees construct, and will easily find their way into the nesting holes between July and November. They all eat bee eggs, cocoons, and larvae, and are only found when cleaning the bee houses.

ACTION: When taking down the bee housing in July/August, place it upright in a protective net storage bag and store in an unheated garage or shed to prevent further infestation. When cleaning in the fall, remove any maggots or larvae and destroy.

Checkered flower beetle larvae (Cleridae)

Cleridae are a family of beetles of the superfamily Cleroidea. They are commonly known as the checkered beetle. The family of Cleridae are seen worldwide, and a variety of habitats and feeding preferences.

Cleridae have many feeding habits. Most are predaceous and feed on other beetles and larvae. It is the latter of these habits that most concerns the mason beekeeper.

ACTION: When cleaning in the fall, (see chapter 6, Fall), remove any maggots or larvae and destroy.

With the many kinds of predators and pests a mason bee can potentially encounter, it is a wonder any survive. However, they do but with varying success. In the wild, mason bee eggs have a 20-30% chance of reaching maturity and hatching. By keeping mason bees in a specially designed house, with active management, you are increasing the survival rate of eggs laid to 70% chance of successful hatching in the spring. Something worth considering when native solitary bees are in decline. By keeping mason bees, you are actively supporting and encouraging the sustainability of bee populations.

Chapter 9

Bee-Attracting Plants

Mason bees hatch early in the year. To ensure that they have sufficient pollen to feed their larvae, they need early flowering plants and trees.

When choosing plants to support your mason bees, remember to:

- Pick native plants. Invasive plants may dominate the garden and crowd out native flowers, which damages the delicate ecosystem of your garden. Ask at your local garden center for recommendations on native, early spring flowering plants.

- Avoid modified plants, especially double-flowered varieties. Many modified flowers are bred for their colours and look, often at the expense of the pollen and nectar. Native plants will provide more nectar and pollen for your bees.

- Vary your flowers throughout the garden to ensure that the bees have a variety of pollen to forage from. Mason bees will utilize any of the flowers available within 100m of the bee house.

- Include plants that bloom later in the year, so other species of bees will continue to have abundant pollen as the season progresses.

- Add plants that bear fruit such as fruit trees and bushes. Trees such as apple, pear, and cherry are their favorites, but they also look for berries and other early flowing bushes.

- Avoid using pesticides in your garden. Any pesticides will severely affect your bees, so do your best to grow your bee-friendly plants without them.

The best flowers for your bees are those with composite flowers and open petals. These types of flower have one circle of petals, which makes it easier for mason bees to obtain nectar and pollen. Flowers with rings of petals and leaves are not recommended, as they make it challenging for the bees to reach the pollen.

Locate a sunny position in your garden where you can create a large area of wildflowers to encourage bees and other pollinators to forage. A small selection of flowers is less likely to attract any pollinators. Include flowers with white, blue, purple, and yellow to best attract bees.

Suggested Plantings

Below is a short list of the most popular early flowering plants that will attract bees and other pollinators to your garden.

Plants and Flowers

- Purple and white lavender
- Poppy
- Crocus
- Hellebore
- Dandelion
- Quince bush
- Forsythia
- Alpine strawberry
- Hyacinth
- Salvia

- Sunflower
- Black-eyed Susan
- Butterfly bush
- Bee-balm
- Catmint
- Heliotrope
- Mahonia
- Daisy
- Alyssum
- Wildflowers
- Any other spring blooming plant native to your area

Trees

- Apple
- Pear
- Cherry
- Plum
- Maple

Conclusion

By the end of your first year keeping mason bees, you may find it difficult to explain the joy of your experience. The delight of watching bees buzz excitedly from plant to plant and back to their house is enthralling and fun. Managing mason bees in your own environment and helping them pollinate is a triumph that can only be experienced firsthand. When your loved ones ask you how it feels to care for them, perhaps your only explanation will be to teach them—at least, that's what happened with us!

Over the past few years, we have seen our small beginnings with one mason bee house and 25 bees grow into well over 100 houses and farms and thousands of cocoons at the end of each season. Our friends have joined in too, helping us create a small army of pollinators. Your simple start this year could turn into the same—with a little help from your friends and family.

In this book we have provided everything you need to enable you to make, operate, and clean your mason bee house, along with how to look after your cocoons and bees throughout the year. We hope that with this knowledge, you'll be able to join the community of people working to bring life and health back to our gardens and our environment.

We wish you many hours of fun in managing your new mason bee house. Happy beekeeping!

References

i. U.S Fish & Wildlife Service (2020, June 15). Threats to Pollinators. Retrieved from: https://fws.gov/pollinators/pollinatorpages/threats.html

ii. United States Department of Agriculture (date unknown). Insects and Pollinators. Retrieved from: https://www.nrcs.usda.gov/wps/portal/nrcs/main/national/plantsanimals/pollinate/

iii. Goulson, D. (2012, October 2). Decline of bees forces China's Apple farmers to pollinate by hand. Retrieved from: https://chinadialogue.net/en/food/5193-decline-of-bees-forces-china-s-apple-farmers-to-pollinate-by-hand/

iv. Wyns, D. (2018, February 8). The Long Haul. Retrieved from: https://beeinformed.org/2018/02/08/the-long-haul/

v. Pesticide Action Network International (2015, July). PAN International consolidated list of banned pesticides. Retrieved from: http://pan-international.org/pan-international-consolidated-list-of-banned-pesticides-explanatory-note/

vi. Conservation and Management of NORTH AMERICAN MASON BEES (*Gonzalez et al. 2012*)

vii. Threats to an ecosystem service: pressures on pollinators (*Burkle et al. 2013, Vanbergen et al. 2013*)

Spring Calendar

Add a photo of your mason bee house location here:

Date house was sited: _____

Location of the house: _____

Amount of pollen available: _____

Pollen types, flowers/trees open flowers: _____

Number of cocoons released: _____

Date first cocoon hatched: ___/_____/_____

Date last cocoon hatched: ___/_____/_____

Number cocoons not hatched: _____

Summer Calendar

Add a photo of your filled (or filling) mason bee house here:

Date of photograph: _____

Additional pollinators seen in the area: _____

_____

Plan for next season's planting: _____

_____

_____

Date Last Mason Bee activity observed: _____

_____

Fall Calendar

Add a photo of your cocoon collection here:

Date of photograph:

Number of healthy cocoons collected this year:

Pests identified within the separable tray house:

Male cocoons: Female cocoons:

Number non-viable cocoons:

Figures and Pictures

Figure 1: A bumblebee pollinating a flower.

Figure 2: Mason bee entering a Reed House

Figure 3: Mason Bee collecting Pollen

Figure 4: Mason Bee entering reed house

Figure 5: Example of Reed mason bee house

Figure 6: Example mason bee Paper straws

Figure 7: Example of Drilled hole mason bee House

Figure 8: Reed mason Bee House

Figure 9: Example straws for mason bee house

Figure 10: Straws in mason bee house

Figure 11: Mason bee capping a drill in a tree log

Figure 12: Example Sperate tray mason bee house (assembled)

Figure 13: Example securing bar through trays – fixed by butterfly nut

Figure 14: Mason bee house at end of the season

Figure 15: Tools ready for cleaning separable mason bee house

Figure 16: Unscrewing the condo to separate trays

Figure 17: A typical view inside a tray from the mason bee house

Figure18: Houdini maggots, close-up

Figure 19: Scrape out and wash

Figure 20: Do not waterlog the cocoons

Figure 21: Wash and repeat

Figure 22: Rinse

Figure 23: And rinse again

Figure 24: Identification of bee sex

Figure 25: Questionable cocoons

Figure 26: Disinfecting cocoons and trays

Figure 27: Cleaning the condo

Figure 28: Dry and reassemble the house

Figure 29: Mason bee house at end of the season

Made in the USA
Monee, IL
02 April 2022